Book #1

MONEY-MAKING SUNNY

by **Darrah Brustein**

Illustrations by **Mike Woodcock**

Finance Whiz Kids

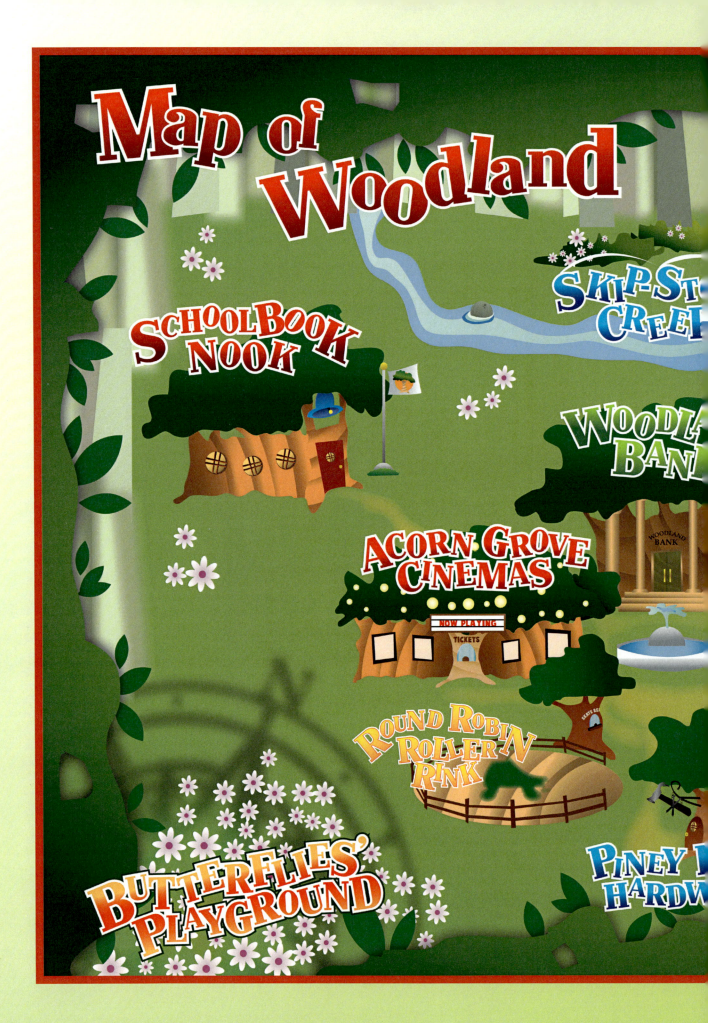

"I'm so glad it's summer, Daisy! School's out and there's no more homework, teachers, or waking up early. This is the life!" Sunny Squirrel frolicked on the bank of the creek, enjoying the summer sunshine. "I can't wait for us to have our best vacation yet!"

"I know what you mean!" Sunny's best friend, Daisy Deer, couldn't tear the smile off her face. "There are so many things I want to do: Go to the movies, and to the mall, and buy a new soccer ball for us to play with."

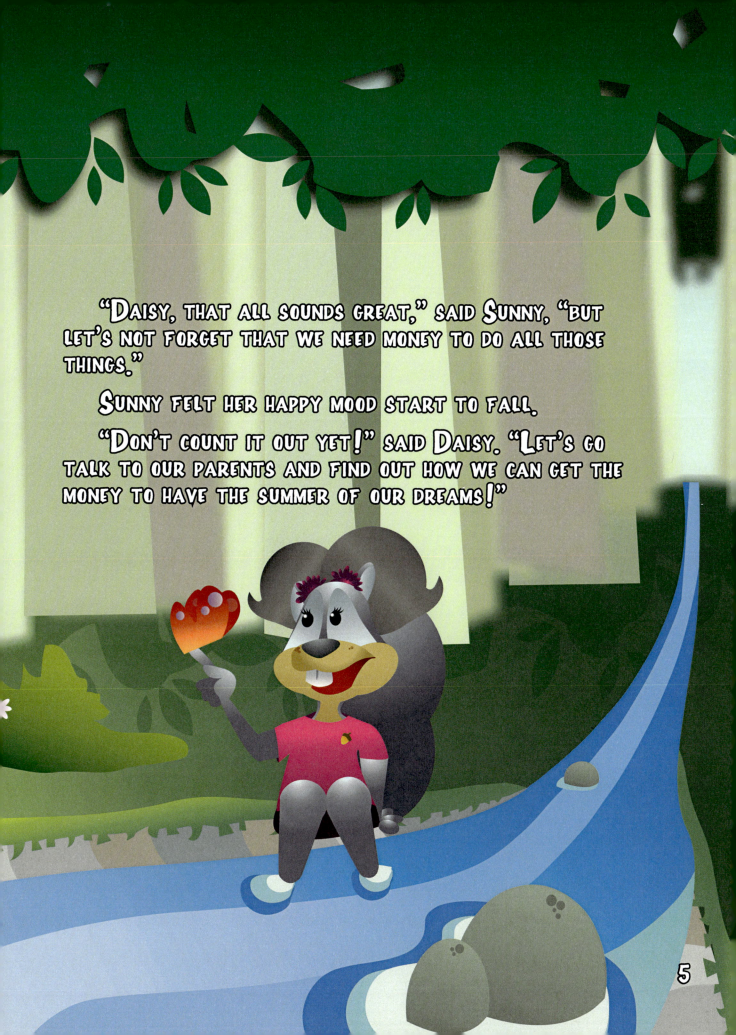

"Daisy, that all sounds great," said Sunny, "but let's not forget that we need money to do all those things."

Sunny felt her happy mood start to fall.

"Don't count it out yet!" said Daisy. "Let's go talk to our parents and find out how we can get the money to have the summer of our dreams!"

Sunny returned to her home in the oak tree, where Mama and Papa Squirrel were making dinner on the stove.

"So how was your last day of school, dear?" asked Papa. "What are your plans for the summer? Some reading or craft-making perhaps? I've got a whole basket of acorn tops you could use to make something special!"

"Well..." replied Sunny slowly, "that wasn't quite what I had in mind."

Mama and Papa peered at Sunny expectantly.

"Well, Daisy and I were talking," Sunny began, "and we think we are growing up. There are so many fun things we'd like to do this summer—on our own." Sunny paused and looked at the floor. "We recognize, though, that the type of things we'd really like to do cost money."

Sunny lifted her head, nervous about her parents' response.

Mama and Papa Squirrel looked at each other and then at Sunny.

"Sweetheart," Mama said, "you're absolutely right."

Sunny breathed a sigh of relief.

"Papa and I have already been discussing this," Mama continued, "and we agree that it's time we teach you about the responsibility of money."

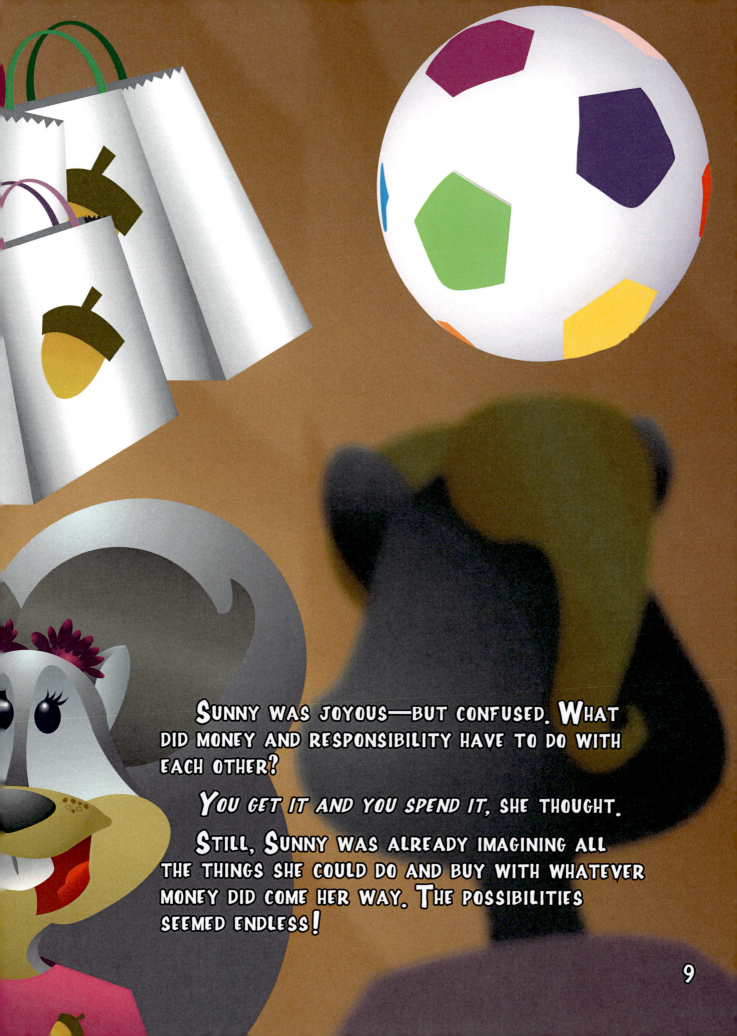

Sunny was joyous—but confused. What did money and responsibility have to do with each other?

You get it and you spend it, she thought.

Still, Sunny was already imagining all the things she could do and buy with whatever money did come her way. The possibilities seemed endless!

"Sunny?" Papa interrupted her daydream. "What your mother is saying is that we would like to set up an allowance for you. Each week, if you complete your chores around the house and treat your mother and me respectfully, you will earn four dollars."

Sunny was so excited she perked up all the way to the tips of her ears.

"But—" he continued, "the amount will be reduced if you fail to do everything we've agreed upon. At the end of each week, we will review your performance and compute your total earnings."

Papa paused, and looked over at Mama. Was there more?

"Your mother and I also want you to learn the importance of savings," Papa said. "You're going to create two piggy banks: one for spending and short-term savings, and the other for long-term savings."

Sunny tilted her head, thinking.

"Let's say you'd like to purchase a doll," explained Mama. "A doll costs more than four dollars, so you'd need to save for it."

Sunny nodded. That made sense so far.

"So...you would use money from your short-term savings bank, which you have stored there over the course of several weeks."

"What's the difference between short-term savings and long-term savings?" asked Sunny. Several weeks sounded like a long time to her!

"Long-term funds will be totally off-limits right now," said Papa, "so you can have money saved for more important things when you are older—like college."

Sunny nodded half-heartedly.

Papa continued, "And short-term funds are for things you'd like to buy now, or soon."

Sunny smiled. That sounded better, but still...

"It's not so bad," Mama said. "You'll see that when you set aside some of your earnings immediately, you won't even be tempted to spend it!"

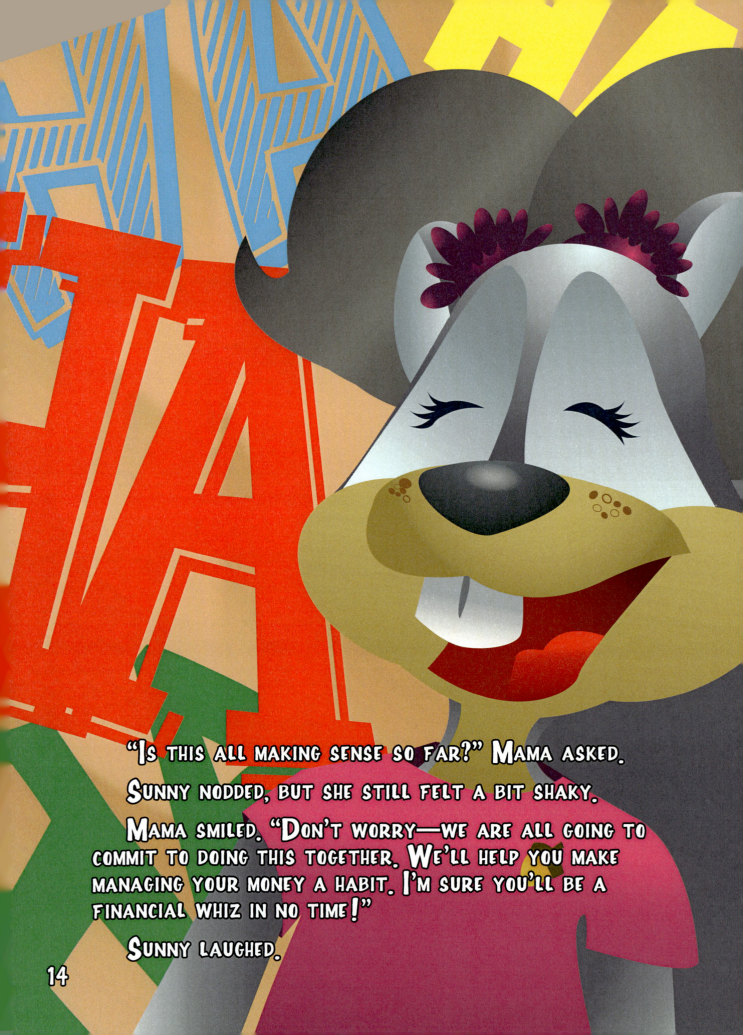

"Is this all making sense so far?" Mama asked.

Sunny nodded, but she still felt a bit shaky.

Mama smiled. "Don't worry—we are all going to commit to doing this together. We'll help you make managing your money a habit. I'm sure you'll be a financial whiz in no time!"

Sunny laughed.

"Can I go tell Daisy the good news?" Sunny was excited to start earning money!

"Surely," said Mama. "Just please be back before dinner. We'd like to sit down and go over the details of how this will all work."

"Great!" said Sunny, already one foot out the door. "Be back in a bit!"

Sunny was greeted at the Deer's knoll by Daisy's mom.

Unable to contain her glee, Sunny started explaining to Mrs. Deer all about the allowance plan she and her parents were creating.

Wrapped up in her own excitement, Sunny didn't even notice Daisy at first.

Then Sunny spotted her friend on the floor, looking a little down. She immediately stopped talking and looked up at Mrs. Deer.

"That's very interesting," said Mrs. Deer. "Daisy and I were just having a similar discussion—but I was worried that if I gave Daisy money, she'd simply spend it frivolously."

"Perhaps I'll give her the chance to work for the money and prove to me that she can be responsible with her earnings. This is a great way for you two to learn a thing or two about the value of a dollar."

Daisy leapt up off the floor and joined her mother and Sunny.

"Really, Mom?" asked Daisy. "Can we?"

At Mrs. Deer's nod, Daisy and Sunny jumped up and down excitedly. Sunny couldn't believe their good fortune: Think of all the doors that would open for them as mature, money-making ladies!

That weekend, Sunny sat down with her parents and created a plan for her allowance, including her responsibilities and how much money would be withheld if her tasks were not completed.

When they finished, Sunny felt good about the rewards—as well as the rules—and she knew Mama and Papa did too!

Week One began on Monday, and Sunny was on pins and needles waiting to start the experiment.

Monday morning came, and Sunny popped up and made her bed faster than ever before! She dashed into the kitchen and checked her chart, which she and her parents had made together:

- Take out trash
- Pick up bedroom
- Help set the table

Eager to get her four dollars for the week, Sunny rushed back into her room and put all her toys and clothes into their place.

"Looks as if we're off to a good start," chuckled Papa from behind his newspaper when Sunny returned to the family room.

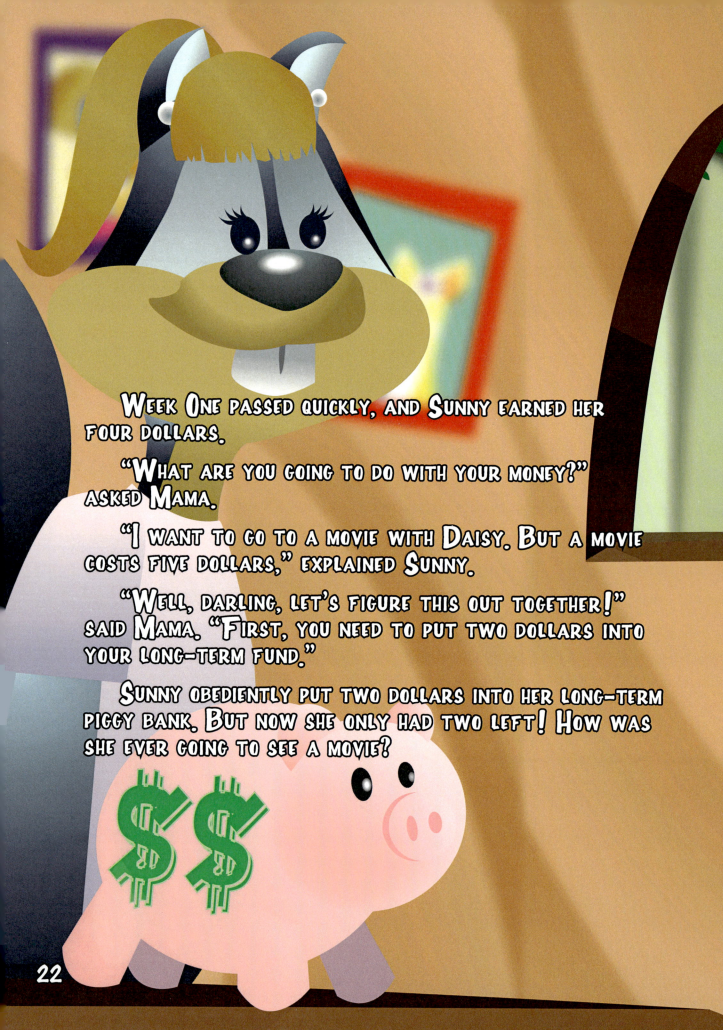

Week One passed quickly, and Sunny earned her four dollars.

"What are you going to do with your money?" asked Mama.

"I want to go to a movie with Daisy. But a movie costs five dollars," explained Sunny.

"Well, darling, let's figure this out together!" said Mama. "First, you need to put two dollars into your long-term fund."

Sunny obediently put two dollars into her long-term piggy bank. But now she only had two left! How was she ever going to see a movie?

"Now," continued Mama. "You have a choice: You can either spend your remaining two dollars now, or put it into your short-term savings piggy bank, which we can call your 'movie fund.'

"If you put the entire two dollars into the movie fund, and if you do the same thing next week and the week after, you will have saved six dollars: enough money to see the movie—plus a little extra."

"Not to mention a nice start to your long-term savings!" said Papa.

"That makes sense," said Sunny, her mood a bit dampened. "I just wish I could go sooner!"

The Squirrel family was interrupted by a knock on the door. It was Daisy, eager to share that she'd earned her four dollars, too! Off they went to the creek bank, to enjoy their newfound wealth.

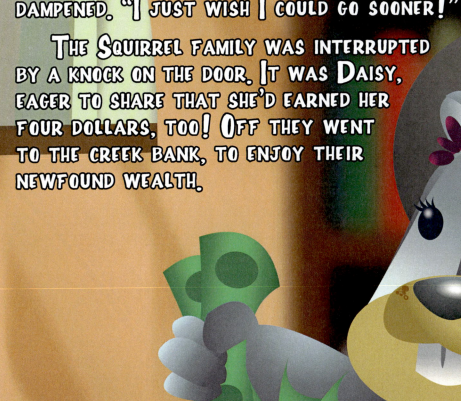

Upon their arrival, a snake slithered toward them.

"Oh no, it's Sidney!" said Daisy under her breath. "I was hoping we could go all summer without having to see him."

"Hello, Sidney," said Sunny, not wanting to be rude.

"Hi," chimed in Daisy.

"Hi, guys. What's new?" asked Sidney, circling them in the grass.

Even though they didn't like Sidney, Sunny and Daisy couldn't help but gush about their exciting new allowance programs.

"You know," said Sidney, "that sounds a little silly to work so hard for so long, simply to see a movie in return. If I were you, I'd spend my money on candy, and then get more money next week and buy something else."

Sunny tried to ignore him. She wanted to stick to her financial plan.

"You know," said Daisy, "maybe you're right, Sidney. I could enjoy that candy now and not have to wait for weeks to get what I want. I think that's what I'll do. You coming, Sunny?"

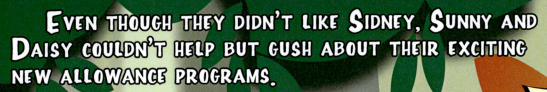

Sunny was torn. If she saved her money to see a movie, Daisy wouldn't have the money to go with her anyway. But if she spent it now, it would be gone.

Mama Squirrel's savings advice replayed in Sunny's mind. But Sidney's simple suggestion filled her thoughts.

"Uh, I guess so," replied Sunny.

The three arrived at Coco Caterpillar's Candy Shop.

Daisy jumped in and started pointing to different gummy candies and chocolates.

Sunny stared at the glass case, feeling unsure. The candy smelled so yummy! She so desperately wanted to taste one of the sweet, sugary morsels.

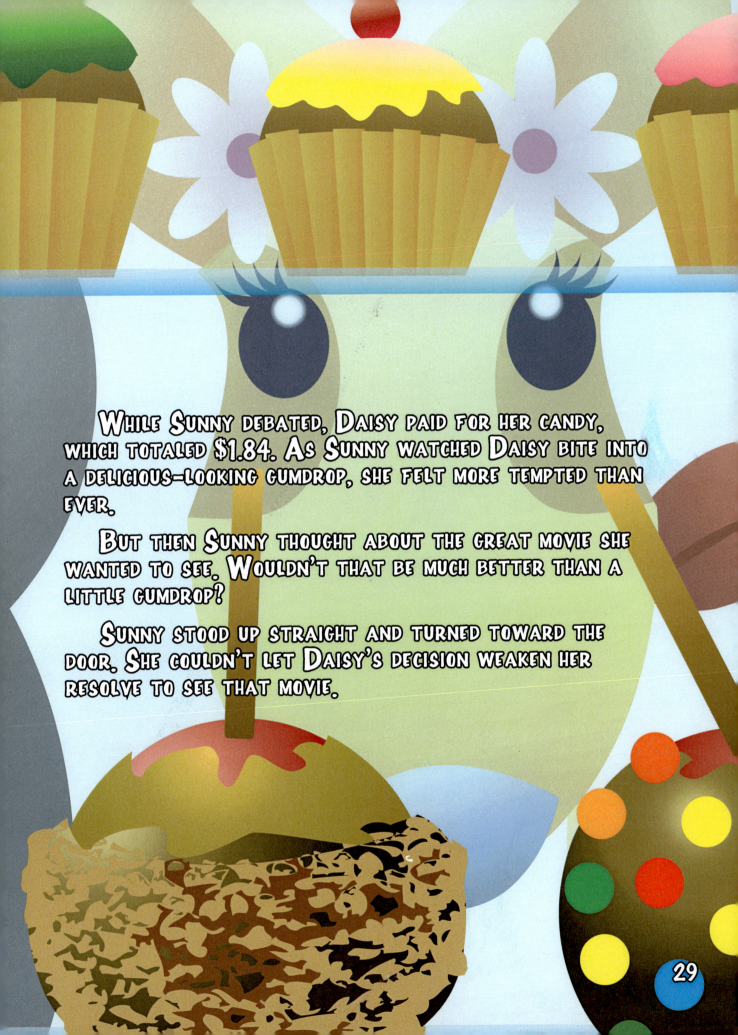

While Sunny debated, Daisy paid for her candy, which totaled $1.84. As Sunny watched Daisy bite into a delicious-looking gumdrop, she felt more tempted than ever.

But then Sunny thought about the great movie she wanted to see. Wouldn't that be much better than a little gumdrop?

Sunny stood up straight and turned toward the door. She couldn't let Daisy's decision weaken her resolve to see that movie.

Outside the candy shop, Daisy shared a piece of her candy with Sunny and Sidney—which was quite generous, especially considering her feelings towards Sidney.

"This is delicious!" said Sidney, "and certainly more fun than saving your money."

Sunny ignored his comment, now even more sure she'd made the right decision.

Once her candy was gone, Daisy said softly, "Sunny, I'm really proud of you for sticking to your guns and saving up for your goal. I'm really sorry that I won't be able to go with you." Daisy knelt to the ground. "Now my stomach hurts from all this candy, and I have nothing to show for it!"

"Wait!" shouted Sunny. "I have an idea: If we both work hard for the next two weeks—and we each put two dollars into our short-term savings, then I'll have six dollars saved and you'll have four dollars."

"Plus sixteen cents!" said Daisy, holding up her coins.

"So," continued Sunny, "if we put our money together, we'll have enough for both of us to see the movie!"

"Brilliant!" exclaimed Daisy. "I really appreciate that you'd share your allowance with me."

As Sunny and Daisy danced around joyously, Sidney rolled his eyes and slithered away. Sunny sighed with relief at his departure.

When Sunny returned home, she told Mama and Papa all about how she'd really wanted to buy some candy, but how she'd seen the bigger picture and decided not to.

Mama Squirrel patted Sunny on the shoulder. "We're so thrilled with how much you're learning already!"

"And how responsible you've proven herself to be!" added Papa.

It felt good to make her parents so proud of her.

Over the next two weeks, it seemed not a day passed without Sidney passing by Sunny and Daisy's spot on the creek bank to tempt them.

"A friend of mine saw that movie you're waiting to see," he told them. "He said it really wasn't that good. Are you sure you want to hold out for it?"

The girls looked at each other, but stayed strong.

A few days later, Sidney slithered in again. "I just had the best ice cream cone ever!" he told them. "Too bad you won't come and get one with me."

Sidney didn't tire of bugging the girls about ways to spend their money on things outside of their goal. But the girls ignored him and, working together, were able to stay focused.

Finally, the big day arrived.

"I'm so glad we waited to spend our money on this!" said Daisy, as the pair made their way to the theater.

"I couldn't agree more," replied Sunny. "In fact all that anticipation makes it even more exciting!"

"I want to see the movie, too!" Sunny and Daisy turned toward a familiar voice. "But I don't have any money left." Sidney looked up at the pair earnestly. "Can you help me?"

Sunny and Daisy shared a glance. "I'm sorry, Sidney," said Sunny, "maybe next time you can save your money too, and we can all go together. But this time just Daisy and I are going to see our well-earned movie!"

Sidney nodded his understanding and slithered back toward the creek.

The two friends approached the box office together, their ten dollars at the ready.

"How can I help you?" asked Ross Raccoon.

Sunny and Daisy turned and smiled at each other. Then they faced Ross together and replied in unison: "We'll take two tickets, please!"

Work Together as a Family to Teach Your Child the Value of Money!

Now that your child is excited about Sunny and Daisy's adventures to earn and save, this is a great time to institute your own home routine! The following ideas have worked for Finance Whiz Kids and could be a good fit for your family, too!

Structure the Plan Wisely!

Here are some guidelines for setting up an allowance structure:

- There are many schools of thought on how much to reward your child. Base the maximum earnings on your child's age and monetary needs. A sample formula is to use the child's age or grade in school times a set dollar amount. For example:

  $5 x 3rd grade = $15

- Clearly show how your child's work affects his or her allowance. You can assign each chore a dollar amount, or pre-determine a weekly total and deduct for any chores not completed.

- Tally and pay the allowance at fixed intervals; weekly or monthly, for example.

- Use a consistent formula, so that your child feels in control of how much he or she will earn and can learn to budget accordingly.

USE VISUALS!

Create an allowance chart to track progress and earnings. The specifics of the tasks will vary depending upon your family's needs and the age of your child(ren).

The most important thing is to clearly spell out each child's responsibilities and to track each day's progress.

Note that some chores may not be daily responsibilities, so mark that in your chart with an **X** or some other delineation.

Here's a simple example:

	Sun	Mon	Tues	Wed	Thurs	Fri	Sat
Set Table (50¢/day)	✓					✓	
Make Bed (50¢/day)		✓	✓	✓	✓	✓	
Clean Room (50¢/day)		✓			✓		✓
Take Out Trash (50¢/day)	X		X		X		✓

Once a task is completed, mark it with a star or fun sticker to provide positive reinforcement for your child!

Put the chart somewhere where everyone can see it. The kitchen is a good place because it's the hub of family life. It keeps the plan front-and-center, as a consistent reminder of both the responsibility and the reward at stake.

The potential for your child to seek positive reinforcement grows as more excitement develops around this focal point.

Once money has been earned, it's time to put it somewhere. Having two piggy banks is a great visual representation for creating two accounts: one for short-term savings and immediate spending; the other for long-term savings. Think of the first as the operating account and the second as the savings account.

Whether to use jars, envelopes, shoeboxes, or actual banks is up to you. Other Finance Whiz Kids have enjoyed decorating their containers as a family. This creates even more excitement around the new system, as well as an additional teaching opportunity.

To reiterate for clarity:

The short-term savings spending bank will be the only money your child can spend in the foreseeable future.

It's important to instill in your child as early as possible, the practice of saving for a rainy day or for larger, more important purchases. The earlier you can institute a paying-yourself-first savings routine, the more likely your child will be to carry this positive habit into adulthood. While it may be difficult for your child to see past his or her immediate desires and to grasp the importance of this exercise, it should be non-negotiable.

The fifty percent remaining in the short-term savings spending account may be used in whatever way your child (and family) deem appropriate.

Stick with the Plan!

Once a plan is agreed upon, what's most important is to be consistent with it.

Of course, these charts can change as you decide what chores are age-appropriate and how the plan works best for your family. It's best to get started immediately and adjust as needed, rather than to try to perfect the plan beforehand. You can start with lower expectations and dollar allotments and ease your way into a more complex allowance system.

Get started today and give your child the gift of learning the value of money!

THE BOOK IS DEDICATED TO MY PARENTS—
FOR HAVING THE FORESIGHT TO TEACH ME ABOUT FINANCES AND PERSONAL RESPONSIBILITY.

Copyright © 2011 by Darrah Brustein

Published by Finance Whiz Kids,
P.O. Box 33022
Decatur, GA 30033
www.FinanceWhizKids.com

Written by Darrah Brustein
Illustrated by Mike Woodcock
Edited by Jennifer Thomas
Designed by Jennifer Thomas

Library of Congress Cataloging-in-Publication Data
is on file with the publisher and the Library of Congress

LCCN: 2011945077

All rights reserved. No part of this book may be reproduced, translated, or transmitted in any form or by any means, graphic, electronic, or mechanical, including photocopying, recording, taping, or by any information storage or retrieval systems, without the permission in writing from the publisher. Requests for permission or further information should be addressed to:

Finance Whiz Kids, P.O. Box 33022, Decatur, GA 30033
or Darrah@FinanceWhizKids.com

ISBN-13: 978-0-9832885-0-3 (Paperback)
ISBN-13: 978-0-9832885-1-0 (ePub)

Printed in the United States of America
Published in the United States of America

Made in the USA
Middletown, DE
27 February 2015